Drawing and Sketching

Deri Robins

QEB Publishing

Published in the United States by
QEB Publishing, Inc.
23062 La Cadena Drive
Laguna Hills
Irvine
CA 92653

Library of Congress Control Number:
2004101531

ISBN 1-59566-045-3

Written by Deri Robbins
Designed by Wladek Szechter/Louise Morley
Edited by Sian Morgan/Matthew Harvey
Illustrated by Melanie Grimshaw

Creative Director: Louise Morley
Editorial Manager: Jean Coppendale

Picture credits
Corbis Rune Hellestad p15
Jean Coppendale p26, p28

Printed and bound in China

The words in **bold** are
explained in the Glossary
on page 30.

Contents

Getting started

Anyone can draw—it's just a matter of learning how to look! This book has lots of techniques to help you improve your drawings.

colored pencils

To get started, you'll need some art kit. Start with a pad of paper, a couple of pencils, and a pencil sharpener. As you learn more, you can try some of the materials below.

Pencils

You need at least three types of pencil: 2H (a hard pencil, for sharp lines and details); HB (medium hard, for sketching), and 2B (a soft pencil, for drawing guidelines and for **shading**.) 4B to 8B pencils are very soft, and are for dark shading.

Eraser

Not just for deleting: you can use it to make **highlights** in your drawings by revealing the paper underneath.

Charcoal and chalk

Charcoal and **chalk** are great for quick sketches, for large areas of color and for adding **texture**.

Oil or chalk pastels

Chalk pastels are soft and crumbly, and give a delicate, blurry effect when you smudge them. Oil pastels make brighter colors.

Pens and felt-tips

These are perfect for strong black lines or sharp detail. The **nibs** come in many different sizes—you need some thick and some thin ones.

Wax crayons

Cheap and good for making bold, colorful pictures and **resist work**.

Paper

Use lots of different types, sizes, and colors of paper. You can make your own cheap sketchpads by stapling scrap paper together. Save your best paper for your final drawings. Experiment with paper with different surfaces: smooth **sketch paper** is best for pencil and pen drawings.

The rough surface of **construction paper** is ideal for pastels, chalk, crayons, and charcoal. The marks on the paper will look different depending on the kind of paper you use.

chalk

crayons

pastels

pencils

eraser

art paper

Get inspired!

You can get ideas for your drawing projects wherever you look. Carry a small sketchbook with you wherever you go, so that you can jot down ideas and make quick, on-the-spot sketches. You can turn these into finished pictures later on.

When you find an interesting object to draw, make a sketch and note its color and **texture**. Texture is the surface of a thing—for example, it might be smooth, rough, or bumpy.

Make an art collection

Collect interesting materials to help you with your drawings. Create a "mood-board" of things that you like, such as leaves, colored scraps of paper, patterns, photos, stamps, labels, and pictures from newspapers and magazines. Paste them into a scrapbook or file them away neatly in a large box. Empty cereal boxes make good art files.

Store your finished drawings safely in **portfolios**. You can make these from cardboard or thick paper.

1 You'll need two pieces of cardboard, a strip of material, some strong tape or glue, and some string or ribbon.

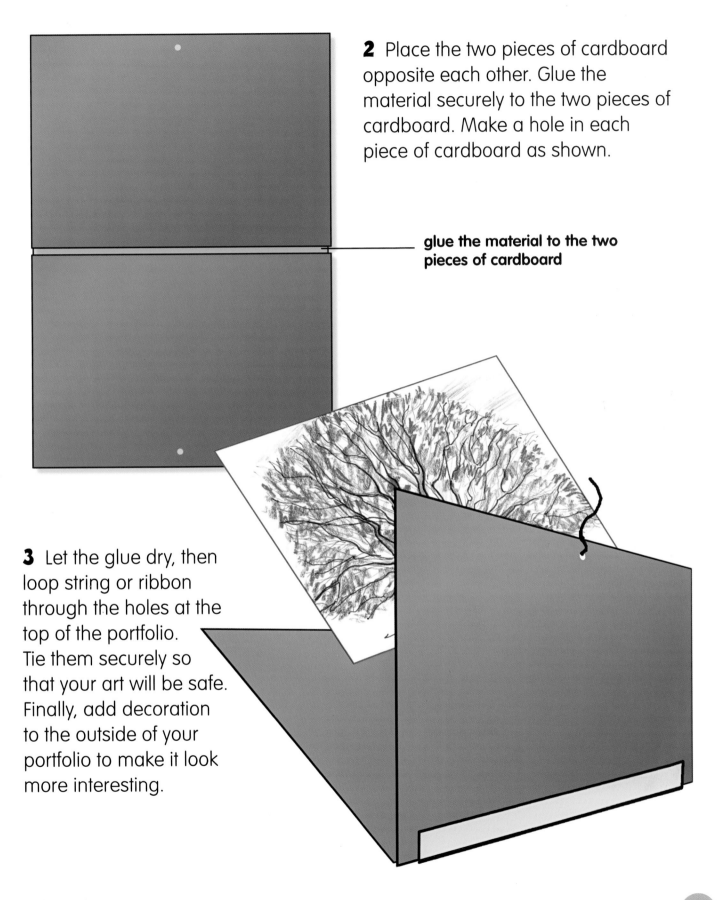

2 Place the two pieces of cardboard opposite each other. Glue the material securely to the two pieces of cardboard. Make a hole in each piece of cardboard as shown.

glue the material to the two pieces of cardboard

3 Let the glue dry, then loop string or ribbon through the holes at the top of the portfolio. Tie them securely so that your art will be safe. Finally, add decoration to the outside of your portfolio to make it look more interesting.

Color and shade

You can color your drawing in solid blocks of color—this makes bold, dramatic pictures, but it can look a bit flat. If you want your picture to look more three-dimensional, you need to add **shade**.

Hatching

This is how most artists add shade and **texture** to their drawings. You can make areas darker just by adding more lines. Try these techniques.

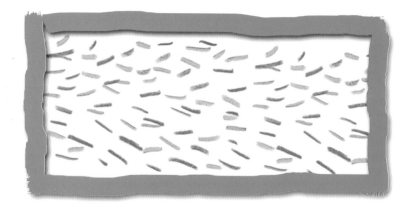

1 In crosshatching, you draw two sets of lines running across each other.

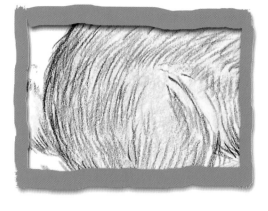

2 Curved hatching lines are good for making shapes look round.

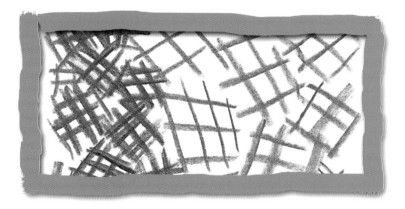

3 Use short lines for drawing fur or feathers. Experiment with pens and pencils.

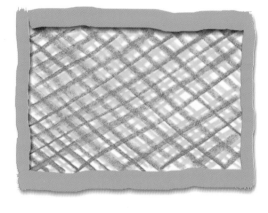

4 The more lines you draw, the darker the shade.

Scribble shading

Small scribbles are good for fast, energetic-looking sketches, such as this one of a guinea pig.

Smudging

Smudging soft pencil, pastel, or charcoal lines gives a soft shading effect.

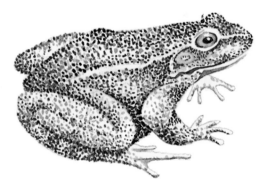

Making highlights

Use an eraser to delete parts of the shading and make **highlights**. This can create pools of light or make parts of the picture look shiny.

Dot shading

Closely drawn dots give soft shade to a picture. Use more than one color—look at them from a distance and they seem to blend together.

Self-portrait

One of the best ways to learn how to sketch people's faces is to draw pictures of yourself. First sketch a quick self-portrait from memory on scrap paper.

Perfect portraits

Is your face round, oval, heart-shaped, square, or long? If you can't tell, use a soft pencil or crayon and trace the shape of your face on a mirror—then you can look at the outline and tell what shape it is.

Before you start your self-portrait, think about your features. What shape are your eyes? Are your lips thin or full? Is your nose long or short?

Follow the steps on page 11. Look carefully at your reflection and draw a picture of your face. Think about the **shading** and **texture**.

Compare it with the first sketch you did—you'll be amazed how much better your new drawing is!

Start by looking carefully at yourself in the mirror. Think about where your ears are in relation to your eyes and nose.

Follow these steps to help you get all your features in the right place:

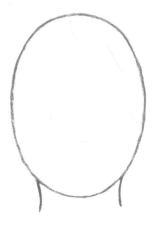

1 Use a soft pencil to sketch a faint egg shape for the **outline** of your face.

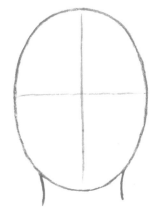

2 Draw a line down the middle of the face, and another one just above the center from side to side.

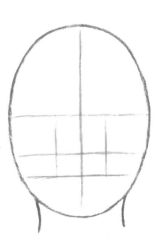

3 Now divide the lower half into two. Then draw three more lines: one across and two up and down for the eyes.

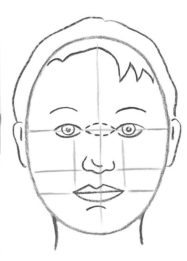

4 Use the lines as a guide to sketch in your eyes. Leave one eye width between them. Draw your mouth: start with the line between the lips, then add the outline of the upper and lower lips. Draw in the tip of your nose, but not the sides.

5 Add your ears, hair, eyelashes, eyebrows, chin, and other details. Now you can add shading and color with colored pencils.

Drawing faces

When you feel confident about drawing yourself, try drawing other people. Faces come in all shapes and sizes, and everyone's features are different. You can build up hundreds of different faces by making an Identikit set.

Identikit set

1 Draw four or five different face shapes, and divide them into sections.

2 Now cut lots of strips of paper, each the same width as the sections in the face.

3 Draw different-shaped eyes on some of the strips, noses on others, and mouths on the rest, all with different expressions.

4 Now mix and match the features on the different faces. You can cut out hairlines, moustaches, and glasses, too.

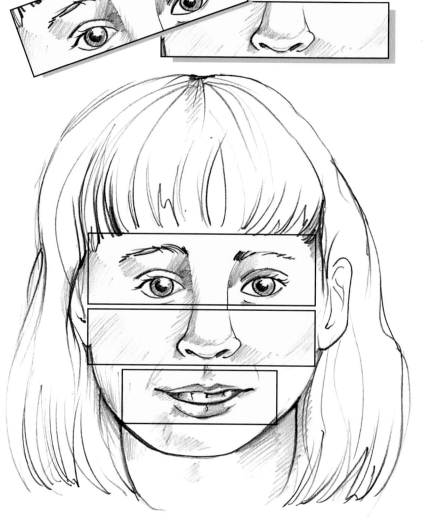

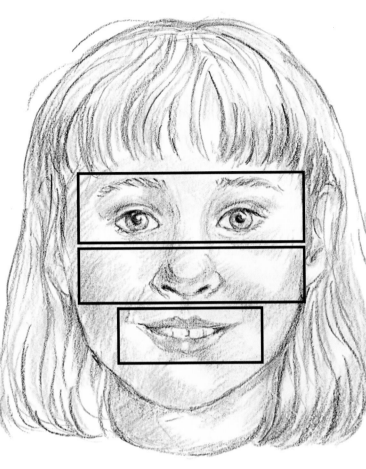

5 When you've created a face you like, trace or copy the **outline** and features onto another piece of paper. Use colored pencils to turn it into a finished drawing.

EGG HEADS

It's not quite as easy to draw people's faces from the side, or from above or below! A hard-boiled egg can be a very useful part of your art kit.

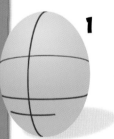 **1** **2** **3**
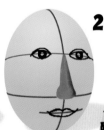

1 Draw lines on the egg exactly as shown.

2 Draw in the features. Stick a blob of clay on for the nose.

3 Using your egg-head as a model, practice drawing faces from different angles.

ART FILE

People don't smile all the time! Collect photos and newspaper cuttings of faces with different expressions, and practice drawing them.

Drawing people

The easiest way to draw figures is to think about the parts of the body as simple shapes. For example, think of the head as an egg, and the arms and legs as sausages or tubes.

1 Start with the head at the top of your paper. Draw an egg shape.

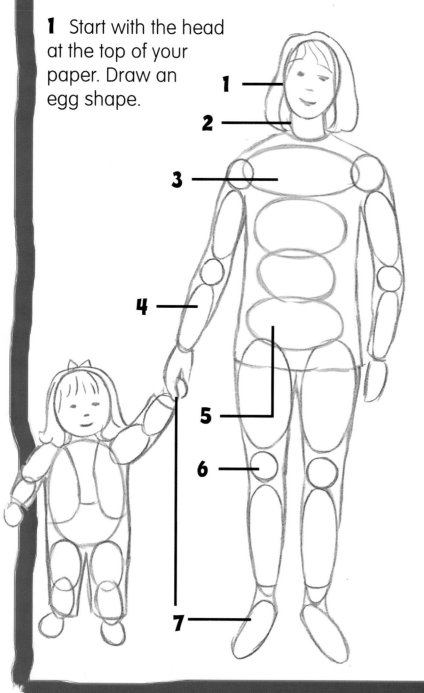

2 Add a short tube for the neck. It should be almost as wide as the head.

3 Now draw an egg shape for the top of the body.

4 Draw the arms as if they were two sausage shapes joined in the middle.

5 Draw the rest of the body using egg shapes and circles.

6 Draw the legs in the same way as the arms, but make them wider at the top.

7 Finally, add simple hand and feet shapes and draw the final **outline** to your figure.

Now draw your sausage and egg figures sitting, lying, or crawling. Look at people in different poses or from different angles to get some ideas.

TRY THIS

If you draw these shapes roughly first of all, you can add the details later. Sketch lightly with a soft pencil. Erase the original lines when your drawing is complete.

Make a poster

Find some photos of your favorite sports, movie, or rock star, and draw him or her by building up from simple shapes.

Use different pens, pencils, and crayons for your picture. What different effects can you create? Remember to use **shading** for the dark areas and leave **highlights** for the light areas.

SOCCER

Moving figures

How can you make figures look as if they are really moving? A number of simple techniques will help you bring your sketches to life.

Art in action

Choose a photograph of someone moving. Make a quick sketch of the figure, using loose strokes. Use your whole arm and not just your fingers and wrists. Try to look at the figure—not at what you are drawing!

Keep your pencil moving all the time, hardly lifting it from the paper. Draw sweeping lines that follow the direction of the motion. This will help convey the illusion of speed and movement, and make your figure look more realistic.

TIP

Take your sketchbook to an event where there will be lots of movement, such as a ball game, ice skating, gymnastics, or dance. Make speedy sketches of the figures. You could also video an event from television. Freeze-frame the moments you are trying to capture.

Practice drawing action shots of sports people or dancers. The trick is not to draw detailed pictures of the people, just what they are doing.

Try using colored pencils to make bold scribble drawings.

Finally, use your sketches to help you draw a finished picture.

TIP

Adding "speed lines" really brings your action figures to life! Curved lines make your figures look as if they are twirling around. Straight lines make your figures look as if they are flashing past!

Perfect pets

Just as human figures can be made up of "eggs and sausages" (page 14), you can draw great pictures of pets by combining simple shapes.

Cat

You can draw a cat from three simple circles.

1 Using a soft pencil, lightly sketch three circles, two for the body and one for the head. Make the head smaller than the body. Add the ears, front legs, and the curl of the tail.

2 Use colored pencils to complete the **outline** of the cat. You can now erase any lines you don't need.

3 Add details, such as eyes, whiskers, fur, and markings.

1

2

3

Here are some other animals for you to sketch.

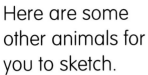

SCRAPBOOK

Collect pictures of as many animals as you can find. Save photos of your pets or of a pet that you would like to have. Collect pictures of your favorite animals on stamps, greeting cards, magazines, or websites.

TIP

Try drawing different types of cats and dogs from photos— or from life, if they will sit still long enough! Remember that heads, tails, ears, and fur are never the same, so look at them carefully before you begin.

Fur and feathers

Sketching the **outline** is the first step when drawing animals. To really bring your drawings to life, you need to add **texture**. One way to do this is to make different types of markings with colored pencils.

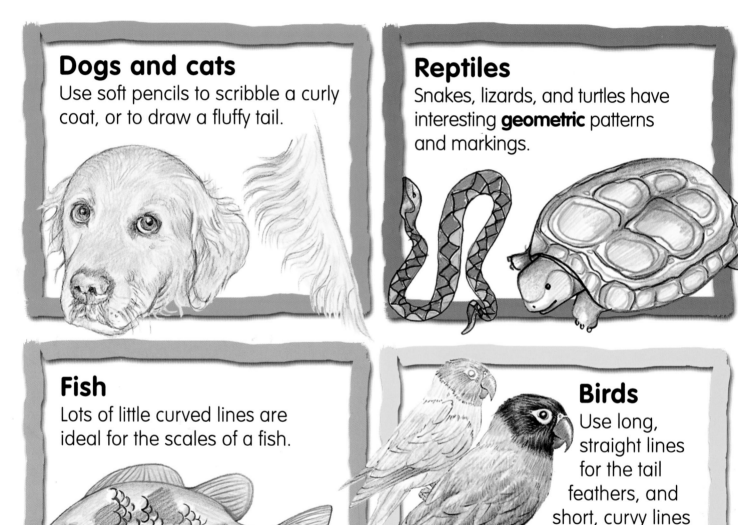

Dogs and cats
Use soft pencils to scribble a curly coat, or to draw a fluffy tail.

Reptiles
Snakes, lizards, and turtles have interesting **geometric** patterns and markings.

Fish
Lots of little curved lines are ideal for the scales of a fish.

Birds
Use long, straight lines for the tail feathers, and short, curvy lines for the head and chest. Hard pencils are good for feathers.

Experiment with different art materials to see which ones produce the most realistic effects for your animals.

Try drawing the same animal using different materials. What happens? How are they different?

Soft pencils or charcoal give a wider, softer effect, and are perfect for drawing fluffy animals.

What happens if you use pastels, chalks, and crayons?

Hard pencils make thin, light lines—great for showing up this squirrel's fluffy tail.

Pens and felt-tips make strong, black lines—the finer the point, the thinner the lines.

Drawing a view

When it comes to drawing a view, how do you decide which bits to put in, and which to leave out? Making a viewfinder can help you to decide.

Make a viewfinder

A viewfinder is a piece of cardboard with a hole in the middle. Make it out of two L-shaped pieces of cardboard, and you can change the shape to make a square or a rectangle.

1 Cut an L-shape out of cardboard. Trace around it to make an identical shape, and cut this one out, too.

2 Use paperclips to hold the pieces together and make a rectangle.

1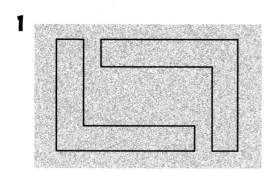

2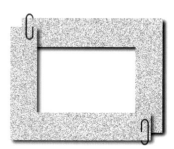

TIP

Silver or white pencils look good on black **construction paper**. Use black pens or felt-tips to draw **silhouettes**—such as a winter **landscape** or a sunset. Silhouettes are solid dark **outlines** on a lighter **background**. They look good against soft white tissue paper or silver backgrounds.

1

Using the viewfinder

1 Hold the viewfinder in front of you. Look through the hole in the middle as if it were a camera lens. Move it around until you find the right view. What happens when you look at the same view **horizontally** and **vertically**?

2 When you have chosen your view, quickly sketch the main parts of the picture with a soft pencil (you can erase it afterward) using one hand . This is your rough outline for the finished picture to indicate large areas, such as grass, sky, or water. Sketch in the position of any buildings or trees.

3 When you have done the outlines, put the viewfinder away and finish the picture, putting in the details and using colored pencils, chalks, or pastels.

2

3

Looking at trees

As with all your drawings, it is important to look carefully at a tree before you try to draw it. Notice how the branches grow from one another, rather than all coming straight from the trunk.

There are a huge variety of tree shapes.

Some trees have long branches that reach out to the side.

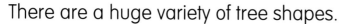

Some trees are are very tall and thin.

UP CLOSE

Bark varies a lot, too. Rubbings are a great way to collect different types of bark for reference. Put a piece of white paper over a section of the trunk and rub the surface with a soft pencil or crayon.

It can help to sketch the overall shape of a tree before you draw in the detail. Try filling the whole piece of paper with your tree shape to make it really dramatic.

1 Lightly sketch in the trunk and the overall **outline** of the tree.

2 Draw the main branches, making them thinner at the ends.

3 Add fine lines for the smaller twigs, right up to the edge of the outline.

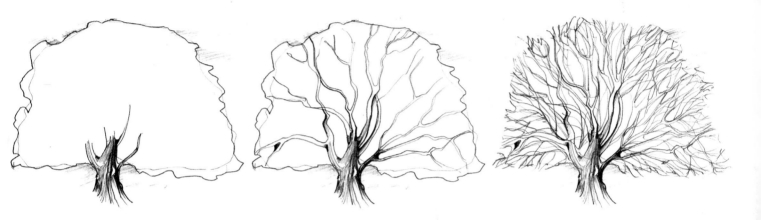

This is how the tree looks in winter, but deciduous trees change throughout the whole year. Leaves appear, change color, and fall; buds can be followed by blossoms, and then berries.

Soft pencils or charcoal are ideal for drawing wintry trees. For a dramatic effect, use white chalk on black paper. Just color the spaces around the tree, and in between the branches, to make dramatic **silhouettes**.

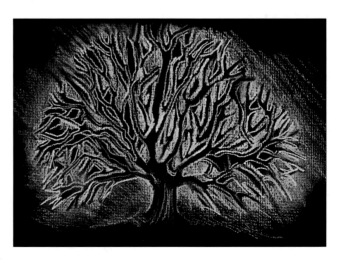

Cityscapes

A cityscape is a view of a city. Don't worry that buildings are too complicated to draw—the trick is to look at everything carefully and to build up the picture from patterns and shapes.

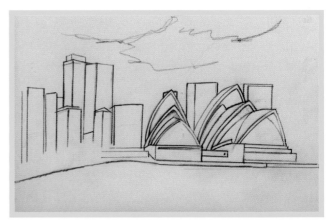

1 Decide what you are going to put into your picture. Are there any interesting buildings in your area? Use your viewfinder to help you decide which is the best view. You could use a scene from a postcard or from a book.

2 First, draw the **outlines** on a wide piece of paper. Look carefully at the buildings—are they wider than they are tall? Do the roofs slope steeply or are they shallow?

3 When you have done the outlines, sketch in the doors and windows. Check how big they are compared with the rest of the building.

4 Add the other details, such as chimneys, turrets, porches, steps, stones, wood, and brick patterns. Finish by adding color, using white to create **highlights** for bright spots.

Build your own

To make a building look three-dimensional, you need to draw its side view in addition to its front.

1 Draw the front of the building.

2 Draw in the sides, to make a **cube**.

3 Add a roof, door, and windows.

4 Shade the side of the house lightly—you could add a shadow to make it look realistic.

1

2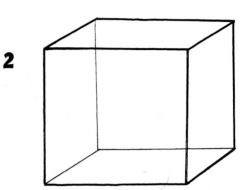

3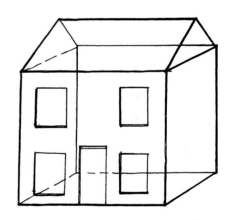

4

Using a grid

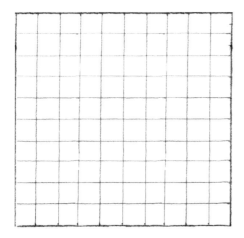

Drawing is about looking and copying exactly what you see. Sometimes our mind tricks us and we draw what we expect to see, not what is actually in front of us. Using a grid can help you get the **proportions** exactly right and can also help you make your pictures larger or smaller.

1 Take a photo or magazine cutting, and trace the **outline** of the picture you want to copy onto tracing paper. Now divide your tracing into equal squares, using a ruler to help you.

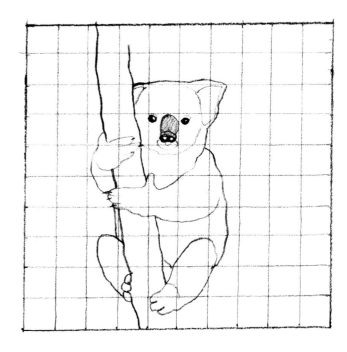

2 Take a sheet of paper, and make the same number of squares using a soft pencil. You can make the squares the same size as the ones on the tracing paper, or they can be smaller or bigger.

3 Copy the main outlines of the picture into each square one by one. Concentrate on each square at a time, rather than looking at the whole picture.

Upside-down drawing

Choose a picture from a magazine that you'd like to draw, and draw a grid over it. Make a separate grid on a sheet of white paper. Turn the original picture upside down. Now copy each square, including all the **shading**. Your finished picture will be much more accurate, because you are just copying areas of color and shade, rather than trying to draw the details.

Using a piece of wallpaper lining, make a big poster of an animal for your wall. Use the grid technique with chalks or charcoals to fill in large areas quickly.

4 When the main outline is complete, erase the guidelines and fill in the smaller details, using the photo as a guide.

Glossary

background
the area of a picture behind the main object—for example, a field and distant hills

chalk
a soft stick of rock used for making soft, smudgy pictures

charcoal
a drawing tool made from charred wood

construction paper
a rough-textured paper—good for chalk and charcoal drawings

cube
a square, six-sided, 3-D shape

geometric
made from a regular pattern

highlights
the bright parts of a picture

horizontal
lines that run across the page

landscape
a scene—such as a country landscape, showing trees and hills, or an industrial landscape, showing factories and buildings

nib
the writing end of a pen

outline
the outer lines of your picture—usually you draw these first and add the details later

portfolio
a case for storing and carrying your drawings

proportion
the relative size of one thing to another

resist work
a form of printing in which you cover a raised surface with ink or paint and then press this down on a sheet of paper

shading
coloring part of your drawing in to make it darker

silhouette
a solid picture that is done by drawing an outline and filling it in

sketch paper
very smooth paper—good for finished drawings

texture
the surface of something—some paper has smooth texture, others have a rougher texture

vertical
lines that run from top to the bottom

Index

Notes for parents and teachers

The projects in this book can be used as home projects or as part of an art class. The ideas in the book offer children inspiration, but you should always encourage them to draw from their own imagination and first-hand observation as well as from memory.

Sourcing ideas

All art projects should tap into children's interests, and be relevant to their lives and experiences. Some stimulating starting points might be: found objects, discussions about their family and pets, hobbies, TV programs, or current affairs.

Encourage children to source their own ideas and references, from books, magazines, the Internet, or CD-ROMs. Digital cameras can create reference material (pictures of landscapes, people, or animals) that can be used with children's finished work (see below).

Other lessons can often be an ideal springboard for an art project—for example, a science field trip can lead to a collection of bark rubbings and leaves, which would make a store of ideas for a landscape picture.

Encourage children to keep a sketchbook of their ideas, and to collect other images and objects to help them develop their drawings.

Give pupils as many first-hand experiences as possible through visits and contact with creative people.

Evaluating work

It's important and motivating for children to share their work with others, and to compare ideas and methods. Encourage them to talk about their work. What do they like best about it? How would they do it differently next time?

Show the children examples of other artists' work—how did they tackle the same subject and problems? Do the children like the work? Why? Why not?

Help children to judge the originality and value of their work, to appreciate the different qualities in others' work, and to respect ways of working that are different from their own. Display all the children's work.

Going further

Look at ways to develop projects—for example, many of the ideas in this book could be adapted into painting, collage, and print-making. You could use image-enhancing computer software and digital scanners to build up and juxtapose images.

At school, show the children how to set up a class art gallery on the school website. Having their work displayed professionally will make them feel that their work is valued.